The Double Reckoning of Christopher Columbus

Also by
Barbara Helfgott Hyett

In Evidence:
Poems of the Liberation of
Nazi Concentration Camps

Natural Law

The Double Reckoning
of Christopher Columbus

3 AUGUST – 12 OCTOBER 1492

Poems by Barbara Helfgott Hyett

With a Foreword by Robert H. Fuson

UNIVERSITY OF ILLINOIS PRESS

Urbana and Chicago

© 1992 by the Board of Trustees of the University of Illinois
Manufactured in the United States of America
C 5 4 3 2 1
This book is printed on acid-free paper.

Some of these poems have appeared in the following publications:
Agni Review: "The Frigate Bird" and "Rain"
The Belligham Review: "The Branch of Fire"
Kalliope: "Before Sunrise," "Gomera," "Thanksgiving," and "Sunrise"
Marblehead Magazine: "Rerigging the Niña"
Sing Heavenly Muse!: "The Widow"
The Women's Review of Books: "Doña Beatriz" and "Isabela"
The North American Exploration, ed. John Allen (University of Nebraska Press): "Imagining the Indies"

Excerpts from the *Diario* of Christopher Columbus are reprinted, with permission, from book #60660, *The Log of Christopher Columbus,* by Robert H. Fuson, copyright 1987 by Robert H. Fuson, published by International Marine/TAB BOOKS, a division of McGraw-Hill, Inc.

The vessels that appear on the jacket and throughout the book are adapted from a drawing in Clements R. Markham's translation of *The Journal of Christopher Columbus (during His First Voyage, 1492-93),* published by the Hakluyt Society of London in 1893. Outline sketches of the three caravels were found on an old map of Hispañola and are believed to have been done by Columbus himself.

See page 109 for CIP information.

FOR NORMAN, WHO SAILED WITH ME

CONTENTS

ONE: SOUTH BY SOUTHWEST

TWO: WEST

THREE: WEST BY SOUTHWEST

FOREWORD

FIVE HUNDRED YEARS AGO, on 3 August 1492, Christo-
pher Columbus and eighty-nine of his companions began
a seventy-day journey that would alter the world's his-
tory and geography, immediately and directly. It is that
outward passage of the First Voyage of Discovery that
establishes the time and the setting for this remarkable col-
lection of poems offered by Barbara Helfgott Hyett during
the Columbian Quincentennial Year.

In a sense, the reader is an unperceived member of the
crew, departing from the tiny Castilian port of Palos on
the same day that Spain's Jews were driven from that land.
Within the week the *Santa María, Pinta,* and *Niña* fetch
the Canary Islands, where conquest, not expulsion, is the
Spaniards' preoccupation. On the island of Gomera the
soon-to-be Admiral of the Ocean Sea waits with his men:
for thirty days supplies are replenished, repairs are effected,
and on Sunday, 9 September 1492, the Canaries fade into
the eastern mists and Discovery Day lies thirty-three days
toward the setting sun.

Every nuance of the outward voyage is captured amidst
the lines of Hyett's poetry: the sea and its moods, the men
and theirs, the ships (one clumsy, one with a malfunction-
ing rudder, one with the wrong rigging), the birds, the
marine life, the weather, and, ultimately, the landfall.

Barbara Hyett's poetry goes beyond the penned words
in Columbus' journal. She has looked into the Admiral's

soul and captured myriad thoughts—some penetrating, others fleeting—that are as much a part of this incredible voyage as the log entries themselves.

The discovery of a small Bahamian island that the natives called Guanahaní (which Columbus instantly re-christened San Salvador) was wholly unintentional. In fact, that singular, momentous event was never fully comprehended either by Columbus or by those close to him. It took another thirty years (and Magellan's voyage of circumnavigation) to reveal the planet in its entire compass. Nonetheless, the landing of ninety Europeans on a speck of coral sand in the western Atlantic Ocean sounded the death knell of the Middle Ages, fanned the flames of the Renaissance, and led to cultural encounters never before imagined.

The landfall of 12 October 1492 transformed Columbus from a relatively obscure character to a major figure on the stage of Europe. It also caused a rising clatter among detractors, who saw him as an incompetent, a charlatan, pirate, fanatic, hypocrite, liar, and slaver. No less often, however, Columbus was perceived as a man of compassion, erudition, courage, tenacity, caution, dedication, and as the best navigator of his time.

An understanding of the easterly tradewind belt is what led Columbus to the Canary Islands as the final departure point for the western voyage. It was also the reason that he re-rigged the *Niña* from lateen to square sails, to better catch the power of the trades. The return voyage, in the more northerly zone of the westerly winds, confirms his comprehension of the wind system. But supreme seaman though he was, Columbus was ill at ease on land and unable to navigate the ship of state or tame the political seas.

It was the great Spanish scholar Salvador de Madariaga who identified one additional trait of the Admiral. In his classic 1940 work, *Christopher Columbus,* Madariaga devoted an entire chapter to the notion that Columbus was also a poet, noting that the spirit of Columbus "had a strong poetic vein, which . . . makes him soar with splendid grandeur in some of his unguarded moments. . . ."

Sometime after the conclusion of the Third Voyage (which ended in November 1500, when the Admiral was carried to Castile in chains), Columbus began to assemble biblical prophesies that might pertain to the liberation of Muslim-held Jerusalem. He called this collection *The Book of Prophecies* and fully intended to set the passages to rhyme. In 1501 he even wrote to his close friend and confidant, Father Gorricio, a letter that is explicit concerning this matter. However, the advent of the Fourth Voyage (1502) and failing health prevented the completion of this project.

It seems appropriate, then, that Columbus' epic First Voyage be commemorated with this lyrical collection of poems. No finer or more fitting memorial could be presented during this Quincentennial year.

Robert H. Fuson

SINCE 1982 I HAVE BEEN engaged in extensive historical research that has served as the basis for much of my poetry. My first collection, *In Evidence: Poems of the Liberation of Nazi Concentration Camps* (1986), derived from my studies with Elie Wiesel at Boston University's School of Theology and from interviews colleagues and I conducted with U.S. GIs who, in 1945, had participated in the so-called "liberation" of death camps in Europe. In the preface to that book, I wondered about whose responsibility it is to document history. I had already completed a second collection of poems (*Natural Law,* 1989), for the most part about Atlantic City, where I was born. In researching the facts about the city, from its invention out of sea farms in the 1850s through the advent of casino gambling in the 1970s, history and memory became inextricably bound.

After the publication of *In Evidence,* I began to fill my historical thirst at the Boston Atheneum with Columbian studies begun when I found, at a library book sale, a copy of Samuel Eliot Morison's translation of the shipboard *Diario* of Columbus. I was searching for a project to serve in the healing process necessary after the awful truths I had confronted in the Holocaust work. Accustomed as I'd become to a full, albeit halting, eyewitness accounting of the experiences of troops in war, this Admiral's journal seemed oddly incomplete. Whole weeks passed without notation. Some days would be remarked by the direction of the wind alone. I was intrigued by the lapses, and alive with questiôns. And so I began to read further: first biographies, then world history, theology, classical astronomy, and geographical accounts of early voyages. I learned about daily life in the Middle Ages; I learned about sailing vessels and sextants and charts.

The figure of Columbus appealed to me: he was forty years old when he embarked on his 1492 voyage, and I was turning forty. Like him, I grew up on the seaside, waking to the sound of waves. The Voyage of Discovery seemed a perfect vehicle for poetry. Until now, all I had known about Columbus was what my fourth-grade teacher had taught me: how the most important of the explorers was looking for a westerly route to the spice islands; how he proved that the world was round by accidently discovering America.

But it soon became apparent that nothing I had learned was so. Not the science, not the geography. Columbus himself was an enigma: among scholars there is little agreement on such matters as his birthplace, his ethnic heritage, even his physical appearance. In the nearly one hundred texts I've read, a hundred different accounts of his life emerge. I joined the Society for the History of Discoveries and began to correspond with some of its members, seeking information or verification of details. Geographers led me to cartographers and they to translators and historians who disagreed about the facts. When a team from the National Geographic Society proposed a new site of the Columbus landfall, archaeologists and geographers at two sessions of the Haklyut Society's meeting at Brown University argued about what spit of what tiny island might have been the first land raised.

Every new book was a scholarly revision; if history was in the telling, I wanted to try. I found a clarifying voice emerging and it seemed to be Columbus himself. Every day I read the books he had read: the works of Ptolemy, Seneca, Pliny, Marco Polo, the Bible. I tried to enter his mind. And it wasn't easy: I was a woman and this was essentially a man's story. No woman sailed. I tried to absorb the human element of the adventure, and the more I wrote, the more I sought to document whatever I could. Oliver Dunn, transcriber and translator of a new version of the Columbus *Diario,* offered me advice about the language pertinent to fifteenth-century ships; Robert Fuson, author of a second new translation of the *Diario,* helped me with the discrepancies in several translations, especially between Las Casas' *Historia* (*ca.* 1565) and Ferdinand Columbus' *Historie* (*ca.* 1539). Howard Zinn, author of *A People's History of the United States,* discussed with me the tragic consequences of the Columbian discovery—the genocide of the Arawak people.

And so I began to see the connection between Columbus and my Holocaust work. My poems were expanding to consider the ethics of the voyage and the nature of discovery itself. I studied Spanish so that I could better read the *Diario* as well as texts by scholars in Spain. Elie Wiesel suggested to me that Columbus was Jewish, and I read the texts by Madariaga and Wiesenthal, who worked to make the same point. I began to consider the nature of prayer, studied Latin, compared the three daily Hebrew services to the offices of prayer for the canonical hours, the Psalms and hymns the sailors sang every day at sea. Delno West, at the Princeton Center of Theological Inquiry, sent me his translation of the unfinished *Book of Prophecies,* Columbus' copybook of Bible passages, so I could study the liturgical evidence the Admiral used to substantiate his dreams of a new world.

Now I needed to place myself in the Columbus world. In 1986 I was awarded travel grants by the Massachusetts Council on the Arts and Humanities and by the Town of Brookline Arts Council and spent three weeks in the Canary Islands, where the Columbus fleet languished for thirty-one landlocked days after the *Pinta* broke her rudder: a month of idleness and frustration were documented in the *Diario* by only three entries. I had come to the Canaries to unearth that silence. Through meetings with members of the history and geology faculties at the University of La Laguna I learned that Columbus' description of mythical volcanic eruptions on Tenerife in 1492 was indeed accurate. I also met with archaeologists at the Canarian Museum in Gran Canaria, botanists at the Horticultural Gardens, and sailed to Gomera with an American team, George Haselton and Eliza Todd, who, with their antique instruments and charts, helped me recreate one leg of the actual voyage.

Two years later I traveled to Spain and Portugal, where Columbus struggled for seven years to finance his voyage. I retraced his efforts: stood in the grand hall of the Alcazar in Córdoba, where he was received by the King and Queen at court, the same hall in which the Inquisition was conducted; I prayed in the synagogue abandoned

five hundred years before by banished Jews; I walked the
gardens of Isabela's palace in Seville, attended mass at La
Rábida, where Columbus and his young son lived, sat on
their bench in the chapel; I walked the streets of Moguer,
stopped at the courtyards, marking the homes of the men
of his crew. In Palos I stood in the dark at St. George's,
where they made communion; and outside, on the hill
overlooking the point of their departure, I wondered at the
dust and the dried-up river bed.

In Portugal I rented a small boat off the coast at Lagos,
rode out, looked back at the grottoes he must have seen
as he swam ashore, shipwrecked; I climbed the jagged
promontory at Sagres, the site of Prince Henry's school of
navigation; in Lisbon, where Columbus worked as a book-
seller and cartographer, I combed the small bookshops by
the city gate; and at the Maritime Museum I sat beside the
Niña's anchors, touched them with my cheek. And all the
time I was traveling, I kept, in bound notebooks, a daily
journal describing what I was learning, what I was feel-
ing, what I had seen. Those entries became the basis for
these poems.

Double Reckoning recreates the *Diario* of Christopher
Columbus, filling in the blanks, the poems accounting for
his thoughts during the month in the Canaries, and each of
the thirty-three days of the outward passage. For Colum-
bus, of course, this was a brave voyage, full of heroism,
fury, fear, mutiny, false signs, acts of vanity, acts of love;
it was a deeply spiritual journey as well. Somewhere at
sea, Columbus, consummate sailor and geographer, loses
the way. It is the scope of *Double Reckoning* to uncover

the meaning and the paradox of the first Columbian voyage to the Americas. Here, at the edge of a new century and a new millennium, five hundred years after East was found by sailing West, I write to reconsider the myth of discovery.

Barbara Helfgott Hyett

ACKNOWLEDGMENTS

I AM GRATEFUL to the Massachusetts Council on the Arts and Humanities, the Brookline Council on the Arts and Humanities, and the Brookline Arts Lottery for grants and awards which funded my research in the Canary Islands; to Susan Bernstein and Nancy Bernstein for believing in this project and for funding my travels to Portugal and Spain; and to The Artists' Foundation, Inc. and The Writers' Room of Boston for a space in which to write.

I am also grateful to Carol Dine for her faithful and critical reading of these poems; Kathi Aguero, Nadya Aisenberg, Lee Dunne, Tom Hurley, Brian Helfgott Hyett, Eric Emanuel Hyett, Jean Lunn, Judy Rosenberg, and Ruth Whitman for advice and editing expertise; the librarians and staff of the Massachusetts State Transportation Library for technical assistance; Margaret Hart for computing and printing support; Fran Wacht for media and information services; Jackson Wright for access to the collections of the Boston Atheneum; Captain George Haselton and ship's mate Eliza Todd for taking me aboard the *Orphus* at Gran Canaria; and, for opening the gates to La Rábida, the Honorable Mayor Pilar Pulgar de Tejero, Palos de la Frontera, Spain.

I wish to acknowledge the following scholars who have generously contributed to my work: Professor John Allen, University of Connecticut; Professor Candido Santiago Alvarez, Ingeniero Agrónomo, Entomología Agrícola de Córdoba; Professor Emeritus Oliver Dunn, Purdue University; Professor Emeritus Robert Fuson, University of South Florida; Julio Izquierda, Secretario de Información, Palos de la Frontera; Professor Lux Marina, Universitario de Tenerife, Las Islas Canarias; Barbara McCorkle, Secretary-Treasurer, Society for the History of Discoveries; Professor Foster Provost, Duquesne University; Professor Delno West, Center of Theological Inquiry, Princeton University; Professor Howard Zinn, Boston University.

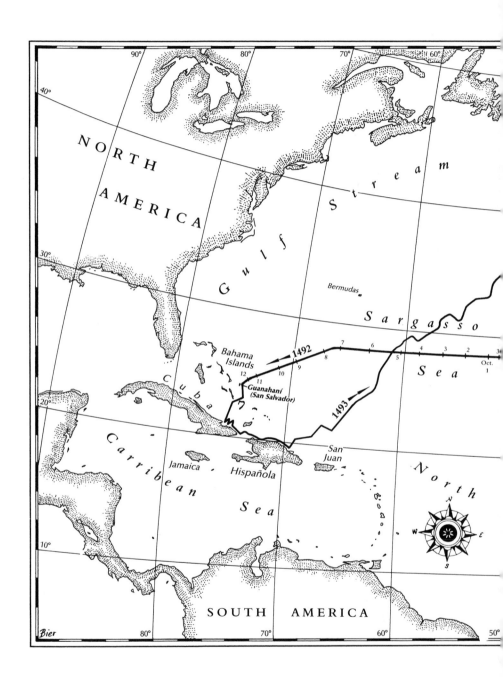

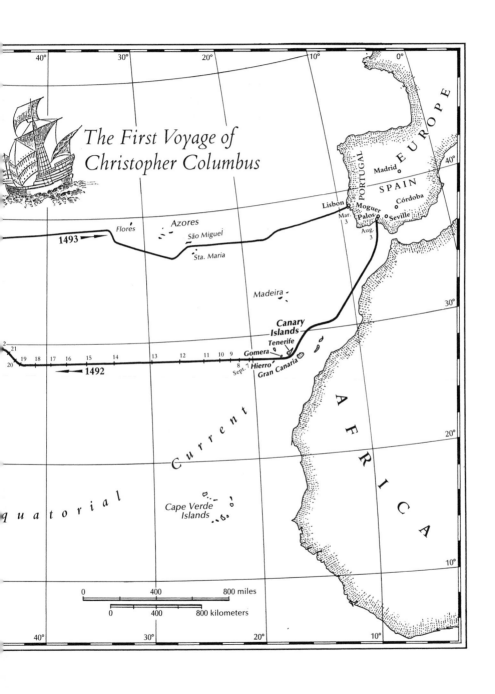

The First Voyage of
Christopher Columbus

40°   30°   20°   10°   0°

EUROPE

PORTUGAL

SPAIN

Madrid

Córdoba

Lisbon
Mar.   Moguer
3   Palos   Seville
Aug.
3

40°

1493

Flores   Azores
São Miguel

Sta. Maria

Madeira

Canary
Islands

Tenerife

30°

2
21
20   19   18   17   16   15   14   13   12   11   10   9   Gomera
1492   8   Hierro
Sept. 7   Gran Canaria

AFRICA

Current

20°

Equatorial

Cape Verde
Islands

10°

0   400   800 miles

0   400   800 kilometers

40°   30°   20°   10°

If at present you and I,
and all our companions,
were not
in this vessel, in the midst
of this sea,
in this unknown
solitude, in a state
as uncertain
and perilous as you please;
in what other condition
of life should we
pass these days?

Christopher Columbus,
Lettera Rarissima
7 May 1505

PROEM: TO WATER

All things in the end return to water.
The sea is a continuum of surge
and yaw. Each time the moon waxes, shells
increase in size. All mountains are connected,

all gods. The waves swell like a pregnant woman
and sails conceive the wind that stirs the weather.
Years follow one another like sheep:
not even the fury of storms can take back dawn.

The waters are cold; jeopardy closes in.
The sun is the heart that constellates the stars
but the same fire obscures them. The human voyage
means nothing to the sea. Every sailor who

breathes is mostly water; and the plankton,
even the flounder that masquerade as sand.
Worms suck at the vents of drowned volcanoes,
the shelves of continents are worn away.

So many sorrows, so many gaps in the reefs.
The sea will wash away distinctions: tide
and shore will disappear. Whoever is moored
will be released. Whatever is done, undone.

ONE: SOUTH BY SOUTHWEST

*We set sail on this third day of August, 1492,
at 8 o'clock in the morning, from the Bar of Saltés.*

—from the *Diario* of Christopher Columbus

BEFORE SUNRISE

Iam lucis orto sidere . . .
Ninety souls are awake and singing. This is
the hour of prime. They can hear the friars' fragile
chant—*et nunc et in perpetuum*—
as they row past the ragged end of land.

Friday, unlucky day of the Crucifixion.
Columbus stands at the bow, wondering,
the way an egret when it wades must wonder
at the circles it makes in water. The sun is

a ghost. He remembers the fountain in the *barrio*
of the Jews. He heard the hush, from behind facades
of doorways, the timbre of a people lost in prayer.
This is the Day of Expulsion. The harbor bulges

with cries: wrecks of families milling among
their animals, children darting like birds
through their mothers' legs, men bent with sacks
of holy books. What he feels is vortex,

or pinprick, he can't decide. He dares not
watch a single darkening face, turns
instead to the mercy of the astrolabe,
the trinity his ships cut on the waves.

We went SW by south.

Saturday, 4 August

TO THE CANARIES

It is always spring in the Canaries,
no seasons to make things change. The trees drop
their leaves at will. Thick fruits at once appear,
eloquent as his parrots in Funchal.

Freed from the cage, their wings green and beating,
they'd fly onto the tree of his shoulders, and stay.
The silver fish that tease the shoreline swim
in small, confining circles. He has grown

accustomed to standing still, consoled by sky
and waves that rock the hull. But how will he
master *Canaria,* the packs of dogs,
the rivers clogged with carcasses and stones?

Do the natives roam the forests naked, their hair
streaming and wild? Or have they been baptized?
He understands the ways of islands: harbors
that welcome, waters that rise to the very limit,

and subside. Soil is volcanic, restless, the way
oxen bear the summer's plough. Green arms
of the cross painted on *Santa Maria*'s sails
seem to become, at dusk, the hilt of a sword.

The rudder of the Pinta, *in which Martín Alonso Pinzón was traveling, slipped from its sockets.*

Monday, 6 August

BREAKING DOWN

Monday is all perturbation. The *Pinta's*
huge rudder has slipped from its gudgeons, unhung.
And the sea is heavy and huge. He comes astern
to hearten the crew, casts his smile like manna

across the waves, calms them with his eyes.
He is a tall man. He wears a velvet
hat. But the men have trouble understanding
the accent of his words. Obliged like Jonah

to a foreign prince, he has appointed
himself to ride the tides, the winds that buoy,
the moon that drives them home. Undaunted, he
is ingenious as nails. He knows how to make do

with what's at hand: release the rudder refusing
to hold; tie up the splinters with ropes. They are
a modest armada, their larder sufficient
with hardtack and barreled sardines. Some men pace

like bears at the Lisbon zoo. He thinks that he
is larger than misfortune. When the wind
listens he confesses sins. To the quarter south
they turn like gulls into the blackening sky.

*The pilots of the three ships disagreed
as to where we were this morning.*

Wednesday, 8 August

ADRIFT

Abandoned by wind, the squadron drifts, bereft
as a one-legged bird: all day afloat
on the same square cubit of green. Calling
across the bows of their ships, the pilots confer,

their voices growing shrill, constrained. They argue
like brothers. He unfurls his charts, draws
a compass with his finger in the air.
He is married to a haphazard crew,

the unpracticed sons of creeks and bays:
Spaniards, Venetians, men of Genoa,
the Portuguese; bound as barnacles are
bound to stone. He must teach them to wait,

orphans before the calm they dread, the sky
without windows. He won't depend on what
he hears in fog, watches instead for the sudden
grace of stars, the legends that hide behind them.

He is like the cables of the anchor, paid out
and secured. He gnaws on the bone of ambition,
wants to extend the vessel of himself,
until he becomes the blue eye of God.

We lay becalmed for two days and are still unable to reach Gomera, though I can see it in the distance.

Saturday, 11 August

BECALMED

He scans the rich green valley, hills rounded
as a sleeping woman's back. The sun enfolds
the wooden deckbeams. The shrouds stay the mast.
He is a tree leaning into wind, a leaf

returning to soil. He scarcely breathes, as if
there were a sparrow on his knee. Birds know
the deep and wandering face of water: believers
in what moves below the surface, they skim

across the sails without regret. They dive
for what is real. He seeks what is hidden,
not just the dawn, not just the cliffs that stand
on the horizon. He can hear the cleats

of soldiers in the port below the trees.
But the wind resists and *Pinta* is taking on water,
sucking like a foal. Taunted by the hips of land,
some of the men give in to grumbling. Some

bathe in the waves that slap the *Niña*'s bulge.
Shouting, they jump off the prow, white shirtsleeves
billowing; they dive. They float like foam,
riding the perfect breath that pumps the sea.

*Doña Beatriz de Peraza y Bobadilla, young widow
of the conquistador Fernán Peraza, and now Governor
of Gomera, is expected to return momentarily from
Gran Canaria with a forty-ton ship.*

Monday, 13 August

THE WIDOW

Heraldic like a banner on the bow,
her long elaborate skirts luff up to wind.
She is a lady in silk embroidered shoes,
her hair plaited and pinched in a sailor's knot.

Widow—what a round and weary word,
as if the wind had named the trees. She thinks
of the first offering of fruit, the shock,
the unexpected loss of Paradise.

She is the keeper of rockcliffs: island that swarms
with lizards and weeds, kingdom of succor and figs.
Her soldiers fight their dragons in their sleep.
She has gathered from the field the rubble

of her husband's bones and drunk her fill
of wailing: the sky ripped into starlessness,
the night wielding its knives. Her fingernails
are wounds. Grief is her body's memory,

the rasp of a husband's lips across her thigh.
She bears her solitude like sheaves of wheat,
her arms stretched out before her in the wind:
prepared again to winnow, prepared to thrive.

There's been no ship from Gran Canaria. I am compelled to lie at anchor, biding my time.

Tuesday, 14 August

AT ANCHOR

And still the hills of Hierro, and still the moon.
He cannot sleep amongst the men who lie
uncomfortably like planks upon the deck.
Their hands work slowly in their dreams, tightening

into fists, or opening like a sudden breach
of whales. He believes in the wisdom of the body,
the skin that sweats, the holiness of veins.
The eyelids of the men flutter and stir. The sea

succumbs to light. He thinks of frescoes in
Seville, candles dispersing the dark among
the dust and ashes that pass for saints. Virgins
and angels dance together on every wall,

not an empty inch: the naves, the arches, streaming
with gilded hair. Halos crowd the altars,
a tumult of white robes and every wing
is blue. He believes they bear him in their hands.

Which is their shadow, and which is his? He studies
the dust of morning. He knows what rebus the blue
sky hides, the stars that burn the way the light
painted into angels burns behind their eyes.

*I passed yet another day at anchor,
still with no sign of Doña Beatriz.*

Thursday, 16 August

ISABELA

Dusk balances upon the mountain,
drops slowly, fades into evening at the peak,
so like the arc and comfort of the breast.
He came to the Queen with a parchment sea of charts

but won her with the piracy of words.
He wandered like a moth from room to room,
every ceiling vaulted, gaudy as a crown.
And Isabela wandered with him, giddy,

twirling in the blue kaleidoscope of tiles.
They whispered on the gilt and velvet couches
in the halls. He could have loved her,
the raven peak of her hairline, her face

chiseled as his own. She gave her smile
reluctantly, her lips abundant as
her gardens: fields of pale narcissus, swollen
lilies, roses dewy as a tongue.

Mazes of blossoms, groves of sculpted trees—
they were lost together in an excess
of creation. They languished there. They ate
the fruit. Their kisses withered in the sun.

I went ashore today to determine if some other ship might be available to me, but none of the few craft at Gomera is capable of a voyage of any length over an open sea.

Saturday, 18 August

GOMERA

In caves, deep in the breathing mountain's side,
the mummies dream. They are the prophets of stone.
He alone is watching giants sleep.
He touches their vessels and their spoons; studies

the afterlife told in paint on the wall.
The shadow of the mountain has become
the mountain. He can't see what it reveals.
His descent to the harbor is steep, painful,

one-dimensional cliffs climbed on his knees.
His hip bones ache. His boots work to plant
themselves like minarets among the weeds,
rankled, the enormous roots of ancient trees,

three thousand years of faith clinging to dust.
Has he forgotton his son, the child he left
asleep, somewhere in Spain? The people here
speak a whistling tongue: a boy, perhaps,

bending his voice above the altar of hills.
His lips askew, three fingers flutter air
across his perfect teeth, calling his father
in birdsong—*Come home! Come home!*

I passed this night near Tenerife, where a great volcano on that island erupted.

Friday, 24 August

THE VOLCANO

O fountain! O black smoke and loud report!
The din as hollow as the sea at storm.
What fat and bellowing monster has lodged itself
in the mountain's throat: the ships in constant tremor,

wine casks clanging as if the hulls were bells.
Lava blisters the face of every rock—
what pith and savagery the earth contains.
The mountaintop has become a smoking plain:

clouds swaddle the crimson sky in gauze.
Since dawn, the glow. The sun has already climbed
the crater, dispelled from every shadow, the echo
of hell: embers, fissures, the smoldering trees.

Hot havoc lay at the feet of Tenerife;
the same black ash that fell on Sicily
falls now upon the men who cower at the rail.
They sail as slow as goslings. They cry. They lower

their eyes, or clasp astonished hands. Ash piles up
thickly on every sailor's shoulder: their beards
are buried. Their feet are bare on the slippery
decks. Like skaters they glide in the pantomine.

I reached Gran Canaria this morning at the hour of nine. Martín had not repaired the rudder. I am disturbed somewhat.

Saturday, 25 August

AT GRAN CANARIA

He believes in the burden of his name—
Christopher—the saint who bore the world
on his shoulders. Tonight a planet shines
the way it did for Ptolemy. The sky is

too vast to change this soon. All day he's watched
wind blow steadily in the same direction.
All day the waves come back. This is the flux
he was drawn to as a boy. Fourteen, and he

saw the corners of his mother's mouth
turn down when he embarked. Ebb tide breathes
the purest air. Bright fish elude the nets
that slacken in the harbor. He is troubled

by the brief betrayals of his men
and by the wound he's carried sixteen years:
sunk into the muscles of his thigh,
gunshot roots inside him like a tree.

His is the stamina of stars. All things
seem possible: the moon waxes, wanes,
disappears, then, one night, reappears,
lifting a skirt to let the light seep through.

I placed Maestro Diego in charge of constructing a new rudder. He is a good man who quickly assembled the most experienced carpenters in the fleet and set about his task with great enthusiasm.

Sunday, 26 August

FIXING THE RUDDER

Fresh-hewn timber, how these boards arch,
a hunter's bow hinged to bring a ship
around. The men envy the reach of branches,
the smell of summer, moss feeding in the dark.

They strip and caulk the wordly boles; they bare
the bark like teeth. The work goes well. The men
give in to cool green shadows, lie down
in the forest, rest their heads on the leaves.

All wood dreams as it breathes, even cut off,
made useable, battered into yardarms
or pressed into the bellies of the hulls: so little
resembling itself. Yet so much pine sings

beneath the pitch and tallow of the keel.
Carpenters learn from the ax, their work as
true as what the oaks believe: *the reaper
must leave something for the gleaner.* Bred

in the curvature of time, there is genius
in stem and heartwood, sap in the rutted veins.
A tree is unencumbered, gentle, possessing
nothing. And when it falls, it turns the world.

The rigging of the Niña *was completed this afternoon.*

Wednesday, 29 August

RERIGGING THE NIÑA

Like the gulls that play the wind at Sagres,
the men are facile and self-assured. They
undo the deadeyes, dismantle the rig,
cut off the points of the huge triangular sails.

The spars keep their sorrow to themselves.
The port is awash with work: the penance of rope
chafing the palms, heat constricting the throat.
The men are wilting. Their skin bruises like fruit.

At his table Columbus sits alone,
leaning on an elbow, tracing his plans.
At sea he measures speed by counting heartbeats;
but fate is the iron heft of triple anchors,

the flukes that tie him down. Soon he will
mount the waves as a graceful lover, coax
the wind past the habitude of land.
The earth is an imperfect circle. All of his

calculations are motes in the eye of the sun.
The ink he writes in is the sea he charts.
He is prepared to be the anxious bridegroom
of a world, half hidden, half revealed.

I arrived this morning in Gomera without incident.
There are many fine Spaniards on this island including
Doña Beatriz de Peraza y Bobadilla,
the mistress of this island.

Sunday, 2 September

DOÑA BEATRIZ

I
The hand that greets his is gloved in fawn.
Still, the touch is damp, a woman's touch,
something fervent in the palm. Her smile
is modest, revealing nothing more than *Welcome,*

nothing more than *Please sit down.* Her mouth
is delicate. He had forgotten the deep ravine
of his heart, forgotten the well a tender thought
could sink. What are the boundaries of desire?

The widow's body strains against the ribbons
at her waist. Her breasts are cordoned and bound.
He is like haze waiting to lift as he slips
between two worlds. He rows to his ship alone

in a gentle rain. He is afraid, not of
the night, but of the longing in his thighs.
His ribs ache like Adam's. He wants to undo
her combs, touch the russet flame of her hair.

He means to be concerned with other things,
but here he lolls on the receding tide,
a suitor at the threshold of his will,
prepared to give himself to this small fire.

II
From the mountains, butterflies move south
before the fall. Nectar still drips from summer
lilies, yet they lift themselves away, sail off,
a flicker in the stained-glass migration of wings.

Now he has come to her chamber, to stand behind her
at the window, smelling her hair. He has washed
his feet for her. She has perfumed her hands.
Now they touch. Such is the dance they feed on.

The roof of her mouth is wine. They are each
the vineyard, each the vine, encircling one
another like the whites of eyes. His face
combs the forest of her body, all mandrake,

cinnamon and myrrh. He kneels above
the latitude of the world. Her ear is
a pomegranate, his tongue is an arrow
from a bow. They are becoming other

than themselves: she is the ocean, he, the sound
of wind. She is the earth, her lips breathing
across his eyes. When she wakes, the valley
he has left in her pillow will smell of waves.

The ships have been loaded and all is ready for the voyage.
Tonight I shall order a special service of Thanksgiving.

Wednesday, 5 September

THANKSGIVING

The men have grown impatient, unhappy
as children exhausted at bedtime, refusing
sleep. They are homesick, not for the winds
of Africa that sweep the plaza of Palos,

but for the promises he made them there,
when the world seemed to rise from his every word.
Now the holds are filled to overflowing.
The kegs and casks are sealed. Even the ballast

has been refreshed with shingle and small stones.
They kneel as supplicants before the dark:
exiled from what is holy in themselves,
they wait for the God of prayers to bring them round.

They are thankful for the storks nesting in
the steeple cross, believing in what tilts
their faces skyward, believing in sky.
When the moon rises in the dusty transept

they do not hear the clang and turning of
the earth. The circle of a day is a psalm:
bless the perpetuity of water,
the deep and teeming stillness they obey.

At three o'clock this morning the NE wind began to blow and I set my course to the west.

Saturday, 8 September

SUNRISE

Another sunrise, a month and a week of fading
stars before he could scud before the wind.
The mountain mocks him with the peak he hopes
will fall from view. He longs to fly, longs to

see the whole world at once, but he is
anchored to the sea. And the very moon
that moves the tides moves him, from one flat
horizon to another. The comfort is noise:

creak of cannon chained to the bulwark, whine
of pulley and sail. At night, the sky resounds.
Now is the moveable wind he has longed for,
the clarion sky. No other shore but what

he seeks ahead. He won't look back, propelled
as he is into spaciousness, an unmarked sea,
a room with open doors. He is beguiled
by mystery, the rust that threads his hair;

yet his eyes are neither stern nor wild with joy—
he would like to be neutral as a monk.
He stares at the rising star of light. West
is not a point to be imagined, but found.

TWO: WEST

This day we completely lost sight of land and many men sighed and wept for fear that they would not see it again for a long time. I comforted them with great promises.

Sunday, 9 September

IMAGINING THE INDIES

All things in the Indies overflow.
Blue cranes throng the marshes. The rivers and lakes
are lustrous with swans. Along the quays, men fish
with gigantic poles and silk. None of the shoals

is dangerous. Ships take the coves like streams.
Musk and lichens swell in the cedar forests.
Past the plain and mountains, marble and dome.
Each crystal palace shines. Each city is new.

Every person lives in an honest fashion,
and the king is sympathetic as the moon.
The Indies are the earthly Paradise
where snakes are free to crawl undisguised.

The whole land is fluvial. Red fruit
fattens beneath the canopy of palms.
Wheat as it ripens sways more softly;
the sea is sweet to drink. The sun ascends

to its most majestic height and every hill
it touches wears a purple crown. Tall grasses
bend before the scythe in every valley
and all the dust that sifts through stones is gold.

Today I made 60 leagues at 10 Roman miles an hour. But I decided to reckon less, so that if the voyage should be long, the men will not become afraid. I recorded 48 leagues for them. For myself, I'll keep a secret, accurate reckoning.

Monday, 10 September

THE DOUBLE RECKONING

Truth is a wall. He builds in it a window
so that they might not think themselves so far
from home. He reckons with reality—
only what serves the story is remembered:

he was born in a watchtower; his father
stoked the fire in his eyes. He learned
the gritty certitude of harbors; how they
rise and fall, how they heave to. He was once

the child of weavers and understands the rough
mechanics of the loom: he knows whatever
comes to the warp suffers. The weft is shuttling
backward, threads raveled like so many Roman

miles. He dreads the rift that runs in torrents
from the keel. The men are unafraid of
a gray horizon, but he subtracts from sunrise
to sunrise, a sea of lies. The sun comes up

by will alone. He wears self-deception
as his breastplate. Truth is a callous sailor.
If he could build his men an honest doorway,
they could remember the light of the farthest stars.

At sunset, the needles of our compasses declined to the NW, and in the morning they declined to the NE.

Thursday, 13 September

THE COMPASS

Tonight the compass turns, all lozenges
and painted diamonds balanced as the world
upon a pin. The laws of nature seem to
change as they advance. The magnet is

about to lose its hold: two needles point
not to the covenant of stars but to
the metal behind the sky. He has come
upon a new disorder. He must mistrust

his eyes. The Guards that secure the border of
the Little Dipper lapse and rise. His quadrant
tries to measure moonlight, but he is leaning
toward a glitter he can name: Polaris,

the Pleiades, Casseopeia—
the window fades and is absorbed again.
The compass, always in motion, seeks not just
the starry visible, but farther, the winds

at the origin of time, where earth pours back
her molten breath to sky. At daybreak, every
sailor sees the sparks. The stars condense
to music—outside thought, outside time.

The men of the Niña *say that they have seen a tern.*

Friday, 14 September

THE TERN

His ship is a dark city. No bird wavers
above the sails. No red beak opening,
no spirits that mutter or moan. Only the stars
to sing as they rise in pairs. Inside the bulwarks

and stanchions of the deck, every arch
is painted green. He thinks of peaches, thinks
of the taste of spring. At the rim of sunset,
he imagines an exquisite rain of wings—

the tent of flight, the pelagic kingdom of terns.
His life lay like a plain behind his eyes:
how he comforted his mother from within
her womb, then went to sea; how he nearly drowned.

All night his eyes skimmed the cheek of water.
Now he aches for a sign in the spit of foam:
the world turns and everything that spins
will come again, again the sun, again

this very moon. The wind will roost on the waves
that crown the revolution of the tides.
He, too, will come again before his fate:
landlessness, the same elusive bird.

Early this morning I saw a marvelous branch of fire fall from the sky into the sea, 4 or 5 leagues away.

Saturday, 15 September

THE BRANCH OF FIRE

This is the anarchy of stars, prophesied
from the distance of the meteoric dark,
remote and disinherited as the dead.
Born in the deep parabola, evolved

in the dusty envelope of clouds, a branch
of fire falls like Icarus into the sea.
The waves that rise to meet the blow divide
into streaks and flaming foam: whack of hammer

and sound, ten thousand fish spill up, surprised.
Not a single drop of water is reduced:
not the mist, not the steam. The men cling to
the ropes and the railings; nothing falls away.

The surface of the ocean seems to bend
at the edge of vision. The earth is trembling, and still
the waves conform. Moths outside a window,
sails push themselves against the wind. The sun

comes up slowly, detached as an island
in the purple sky. The men fall silent
and calm. They watch, again, the sky catch fire
and make of this a miracle, a sign.

The weather is like April in Andalusia with mild breezes, and the mornings are delightful.

Sunday, 16 September

APRIL IN ANDALUSIA

God lacks for nothing in Andalusia—rivers
run wild like stallions; nightingales flock to the trees.
In Córdoba the sun consoles the empty
Synagogue. Mosaics sweep the Gates

of Absolution; in the Mosque, a forest
of jewel and filigree, and a wooden crucifix
that hangs in the Cathedral's marble heart.
The whole city is a ministry of ramparts,

an architecture of icons and painted shrines—
God of the Romans, God of the Moors, God
of the Visigoths, God of the Inquisition,
whatever spirit sailors call on, wanders

like a nomad here. In the streets: the blind,
the orphans who beg for coins. The breeze is moist.
The dawn is ruby and lush. Patios gleam
with whitewash and tile; pools teem with carp.

Stairs of the palace wind to the parapets:
vista of gilded archways and polished stones.
The walls of the city yearn for something inside
the decoration, something that God will forgive.

I saw a great deal of weed today—some looks like river grass and the crew found in it a live crab which I kept.

Monday, 17 September

SARGASSO SEA

They sail upon the copse of weed, a shallow
wilderness, a sea of seeds: mottled
undergrowth and swollen branches torn away,
they think, from land. The ship's boy picks a berry,

pinches it, lets air spurt into air.
Even before the earth gave way to land,
this hiss and hum, the oceanic grasses
bursting like the sun. Everything is

reaching toward what comes before the dark
that separates one sailor from another,
sea from sky. This is the human franchise:
how small the mound of earth that covers a grave.

Seaweed propagates itself by portion:
at one end, fruit, and at the other, dying
leaves. Sargassum offers no resistance.
A crab can cut it sideways with a claw

as wizened as the faces of the drowned—
the flattened brow, how the jaw gives in,
how teeth and sunken flesh marry bone.
Even the longest voyage ends too soon.

This day Martín Alonso with the Pinta
*did not wait for the others because he said that he
had seen a great flight of birds moving westward.*

Tuesday, 18 September

THE FLIGHT OF BIRDS

In nature there is always the exception.
Squid swim backwards. Storks are mute. Hawks
can only scream. Out here, the birds swing west
from memory. They navigate by what

they dream, holding dusk in one ear, and in
the other, dawn. *We can ill afford
to come apart this far from home. Pinta*
speeds ahead. Her men forsake the maps

they've memorized, and bless themselves, bowed
by the dusky forest of wings. He sails behind,
his heart as still as a stone. He wants to be
less human: only ecstasy and flame.

He hums the harmony his mother wove
every evening. He might have been a weaver
but for dusk, the unremittance of waves.
All of his years he has lived this fiercely,

hostage to the hunger in his soul.
The ransom will be paid with somebody
else's blood. He spreads his arms, embraces
destiny, the roseate stain of wings.

*Very early this morning, three little birds flew over the
ship, singing as they went, and flew away
as the sun rose.*

Thursday, 20 September

MORNING

All things are opening to him, and none:
this morning, the lightest air, hurled from the highest
branch of sky; three little birds, as modest
as Noah's dove. He weighs the wind their throats

disperse with sound. He is too practical
to be surprised, too steeped in books to learn
what's wholly new. His eyes are locked on ancient
paling stars. He believes that sea birds sleep

on the lip of land and feast from the waves at dawn.
Drizzle of rain: he furrows his brow, casts
a dipsey weight into the deep, finds
the bottom fathomless. How many oceans

wide? Beyond the breach and magnitude
of sea and sky, spokes in the wheel of morning—
the voice of birds, two hundred million songs.
This is the real migration. There is no placé

that he calls home. He envies no one, calls no one
friend. What can be given? What can be taken
away? He is secure in the singular—
rainspout, whirlpool, total eclipse of sun.

I saw a whale, which is another sign of land.

Friday, 21 September

THE WHALE

What rich milk has fed the beast to size?
The whale ascends to show its marbled face,
glides beside him like a twin, its human
eye gleaming, its breath as warm as tears.

Entwined in weeds, it is a sacred thing—
hairless and earless, the billowing folds of skin.
The men fall silent before the wings of flukes.
In the glut of noon, a blowhole spews a fountain

upon its head. How easily it rises
to the surface, how quickly it withdraws,
reconciled like the sun to plunge and rise
again, filling the lungs' cathedral with air.

It can sink a fleet of ships, ramming the hulls
with its sleek sides, turning the decks to matchwood
or straw. Yet it feeds on the smallest creatures that fall
through the net in its jaw as it proceeds, open-eyed,

afraid of tentacles, afraid of sharks.
He, too, is betrayed by what he feels—the blood
that pounds the anvil of his heart. He pities
the handiwork of God, pities the whale.

This contrary wind is of much use to me, because my people were much excited at the thought that in these seas no wind ever blew in the direction of Spain.

Saturday, 22 September

THE CONTRARY WIND

They've had too much of ease, too much of scudding
free before the wind. Now the waves get up
from westward, zone in which there are no
winds at all. They move across the markings

of his charts: the parallel appointed:
no misplaced islets, no hurricanes, no calms.
Hope is a fleur-de-lis fixed to the compass—
dead-reckoned, the course, one straight line out.

He won't fall back. He stands in the wind until
knees ache and the weight of his body yearns
to give up the watch, to rest. He pretends to
want what goes against him, needing nothing

more than what he has, or is about to
have. Even the sun obeys a progress
not its own. The wind comes from the wrong
direction, thrumming the lanyards like a harp.

Vanity drags at his heels—there are wreaths
to be awarded, ribbons, the blushing pomp
of fame. He was not content among the nods
of noblemen. He covets the trophy of stars.

The high sea is a sign which has not appeared except in the time of the Jews when they left Egypt and complained against Moses, who took them out of captivity.

Sunday, 23 September

HIGH SEAS

And the sea rose and the sky became a wall.
The wind reached the mizzenmast and stopped.
Three ships yaw into a swell as high
as a pyramid. What God has lifted the deep

into folds? A pillar of clouds thickens and steams.
Nothing is so violent as the fist of water:
without reason, without restraint. The sails
hang suspended in waves as hard and green

as biblical jasper. The moon returns to its mirror.
Out here, the blaze of morning sings. He knows
some of the secrets of the world. Holding
lodestone to the compass, he feels iron

attract its kind. Everything clings to something:
even the bread of affliction was meant to rise.
East wind is a chariot roiling water,
the spray that scrapes the sky as hard as ice.

His eyes are nearly closed, right hand tensed
like the rod of Moses, daring the sea to part.
The ship beneath him pitches and heaves. But he
stands firm, his legs apart. He is the wave.

At sunset, Martín mounted the stern of the
Pinta *and with great joy called to me,*
"Land, land, sir! I claim the reward."

Tuesday, 25 September

FALSE LANDFALL

The rigging is full of sailors, ladders lost
in the press of men spanning the ropes as ivy
greens the stones of a wall. They've climbed to see
what's left between the Indies and the sea.

Dusk turns their shadows black against the sky.
The ships are bobbing like cork, and what sunlight
gathers on the ship's back is pulled away.
Each man's face is a promise, every eye

staring as if sea were a houseful of jewels.
Night offers its reward in stars. The crow's nest
swoons. Halyards bristle and snap; the strops
sweat in their blocks. Moon is a slit in the sky.

The men dangle precipitously from the ledge
of hope. Wind sinks the virgin forests.
Gloria in excelsis Deo—
fruit trees! Orchards of trees! The strong hands

of men knot in pain. The soles of their feet
clasp the ropes and bleed. They are dogged,
the haughty shrubs that hug the edge of things,
dark and rugged and windswept, holding on.

After sunrise I realized that what we all thought was land last evening was nothing more than squall clouds.

Wednesday, 26 September

AFTER SUNRISE

Whitecaps rise like blossoms on the waves.
He thinks of the splendor of Spain: extravagant
boulevards, balconies, lark and jasmine,
hinds grazing the tapestries in the hall.

Sea is an illuminated manuscript,
ripe with emerald fish whose scales are gold.
He thinks of dew making pearls in Pliny's oysters,
the inaccessible bounty of shells. Even

wind can't lull this dream asleep. At every
shore waves lap the tideline. Yet thirst will
not be satisfied. His men feed on the fish
they spear, but he is insatiable as prayer.

He imagines the first sight of land: at daybreak,
jagged and faint the way a smile creases
the eyelids of a girl. He watches the light:
first, the shadows skittering like swallows,

then the sheen. He is aware of the knot
that tightens his shoulder. He takes off his hat,
undoes the buttons of his shirt, his heart undressed,
trembling like the flame inside the sun.

This morning I saw a bird that is called a frigate bird, which makes terns throw up what they have eaten in order to eat it herself, and she does not sustain herself on anything else.

Saturday, 29 September

THE FRIGATE BIRD

How does a bird explain the sorrow of
the world, the grind and scrape of bodies, the stern
tenacity of bone? Climbing, or asleep
and hovering, there is a creature as still

as a statue, a black star painted in the sky.
Its brain is smaller than a fingertip,
and though its great hooked bill is fierce, its feet
are weak. It floats in space as slow as a plume

of smoke, then hurtles in a streaking dive.
It stops, an inch above the waves, afraid
of the shock of water, its own capacity
to drown. The rhythmic clacking of the beak

awakens a hostile need. From what it has
to what it wants, and back again, it swirls,
swipes, buffeting the terns in thrusts
and stabs. Once the frigate bird has fed,

its eye is as docile as a nun. Dwarfed by
the light that vaults the distance, obedient
as the whim of clouds to wind, it disappears,
as blameless as a soul without belief.

It rained very hard this morning.

Monday, 1 October

RAIN

Most of his life is gone, spent far from land
and bed and comfort. Cold rain spills upon
the lashes of his eyes. All waters run.
The sea drags from the sea its equal self.

The not-yet-born carry charts within
their liquid minds. It takes a year to build
a caravel; just an hour to bring it
down. The sky is a dark sea and churning.

The lombards and the muskets fill with water.
Everything is flooding: the portholes and
the buckets, the binnacle, the swollen clouds.
Thick fog blunts the sky; the mainsail sags.

On the surface of the wind, the tallest waves
totter and drown. The whole world is brimming.
And while the hull leaks like a wicker basket,
and his legs are sunk in rainwater to the knees,

he hears beneath the rolling of his ship
a gentler surge—the exhalation and pulse
of memory, the waters from which he once
emerged: head first and dreaming, like a seed.

There are many fish and the crew killed one.

Tuesday, 2 October

THE KILL

He thinks that he despises violence: war,
the open jaws of beasts. He is sulking,
dispirited as the air in his cabin,
tired of this weak-kneed reaching for what's left

on the olive branch, tired of the crumbs,
of his service to the night. He resurrects
the bleeding fish, its thick gills blackened
as thunder, eye smashed like a potter's jug.

The course he holds is fragile. The moon stipples
the yards, light moving from mast to mast
like brittle birds. The stars rise pale as deer.
Even if the wind is full and vicious, the stars

will rise, the waves will roll relentlessly
beneath the surface, steadfast, reclaiming their kind.
He will bind the world but not belong to it:
there will be no fruits of his old age.

He lies on his bed, granitic in the dark.
The world will dissolve one day, he has prepared
himself for this. The fish is the warning.
The sea is a fresh grave covered with bouquets.

There is more weed, but it is withered and appears old.

Wednesday, 3 October

WEEDS

He would like to be Odysseus, tied to
the mast, seduced by nothing, not the weed,
not the rotting stems. Everywhere
this coming and this going, the principle

of fortune, the gravity beneath the tides.
How to remember dawn in October,
every speck and shard of light, so many
trimmings of water lent to wind? His life

has been a welt of heavy blows, yet he
is as stable as the cooper at his bench.
Endure. Endure. Happiness is just
another end, human and imperfect

as the moons that crest his fingernails. These, too,
will wither and decay. The real moon bends
the light that glances off the waves. The night
is turning inward, its dark eye staring back.

He watches with a sailor's modesty the clouds
that hallow sunrise, the sky disrobing, slowly
becoming day. He aspires to the vestments
of eternity: the perfumed shroud of kings.

*More than 40 petrels came to the ship
at one time, and with them two boobies;
a boy of the caravel hit one with a stone.*

Thursday, 4 October

THE STONE

Idleness has made a boy a killer,
reconciled to the mortal: the shudder and crack
of bone. A single stone has taught the birds
to weep. The ships follow the course of their making.

The machine of daily living turns and grinds:
they carry the ocean bottom with them, stinking
in the tarred and oakum holds: bilge water,
sand and gravel, ballast of dusty stones.

Every day is the measure of small deaths,
and every night, immeasurable dying stars.
Monotony is a mean-spirited master:
the men have grown indignant, made hollow

by the impulse to be cruel. The sea runs swiftly.
The ropes and the knots tend to themselves. In good
weather there's little enough for a sailor to do.
The sky's as empty as the sneer of God.

The wind is a dirge in the white waft of feathers.
A stone has shattered the skull of a bird into beads.
The sea is grieving. The waves rend their garments.
Fish feed on bread and the ashes of the heart.

Many flying fish flew aboard the ship.

Friday, 5 October

FLYING FISH

Gunshot, a flock of fish spills up from the sea,
a spate of shadows suddenly made real.
Without muscles in their wings, they lift
themselves from water, tails rooted in waves.

Fish that can stand on water! Fish that can sail
on the furl of their silver fins! These are
the spindled beasts of middle air, intimate
with speed and sky and wind. They are drawn

to the lights of ships where men gather in circles
around the raw sienna heat of fires;
sailing men, in red wool caps, emboldened
by fish that fly. What falls to the deck is returned

to water; the sky empties itself of scales.
At the boundaries of the elemental world
the ships mark the waves like skipping stones,
their substance beating ocean into foam.

But fish ride the cleft between sea and air,
the double habitat where they have been thrust,
their keeled bodies racing through water, faster
than any ship, more plentiful and higher.

This evening Martín Alonso Pinzón told me that he thought it would be wise to steer to the SW by west in order to reach the island of Cipango. In my opinion it is better to continue directly west until we reach the mainland.

Saturday, 6 October

CIPANGO

The horizon cuts its oar into the sky.
What is visible appears far. He knows
from charts the mountains that rise from the south,
and every mountain slows the wind. It is calm;

the birds expected dark an hour ago.
Out there is an island of well-mannered people—
their emperor is just. Their dead are buried
with pearls in their mouths. Their idols have heads of dogs

and cattle, and some have a thousand hands. He expects
the unexpected: doubt recedes like the coast
in fog. He has departed from ports in darkness,
and sailed through coral reefs. Now Cipango

lifts its mythical eye; he will not be
moved. He will hold his course until a new
sea will wash away misgiving and he
will be saved: he does not believe in luck.

There is danger in every wave that shears
the water, but his soul is too buoyant to drown.
The things he seeks have been set before him.
The moon is his mistress. He watches her rise.

Joy turned to dismay as the day progressed, for by evening we had found no land. God did offer us, however, a small token of comfort: many large flocks of birds flew over.

Sunday, 7 October

THE TOKEN

Breakfast is a salty biscuit, a piece
of cheese. He leans on the rail, studies the silver
squid that braid the sea. Sound shreds the fabric
of morning: a bird utters a cry to its kind.

Multitudes of birds: the ships of their bodies
are compasses, the hulls of their minds are clocks.
Twelve miles into daylight and the prows point south.
The men on the decks bathe in the shadow of flight.

The sky is a meadow; the sea, an orchard groaning
with fruit. The men work up a hatred and brood.
They long for privacy, some space around
the body, the individual tide of sleep.

The birds are exuberant. They share one dream.
Their feathers are constantly growing, constantly
falling away. The sky is a jeer of birds,
coming together like haze to hide the sun.

The watch is set. The gromet turns the glass.
How many birds until landfall? Enough
to teach the men to live together below,
in harmony, breathing the same stale air.

THREE: WEST BY SOUTHWEST

The sea is like the river in Seville, thanks to God, and the breezes, as sweet as in April in Seville, so that it is a pleasure to be in them, they are so fragrant.

Monday, 8 October

BREEZES

He breathes the elegant air, studies the clouds
that tell no more, no less, than yesterday;
the sea so calm a full-sailed caravel
might be a swan. The men toss ballast stones

onto the waves and watch the froth snap back;
the birds embrace their arcs. On the Guadalquivir,
birds roost on the chain that spans the river.
He tasted sweetness there, renewed himself

in the murmured counsel of water. The sun swings low.
The air is soft—he yearns for hills: how
the horns of heifers turn to gold in April,
how the stalks of saffron crocus sway.

The sky is a nosegay; the scent as welcome as wine.
He depends on the breeze, and on the sensual feel
of the tiller. His breath sours with loneliness;
his fingers touch shadows beneath his eyes.

At last, he lifts the kerchief of his gaze—
the sea is smooth as the wrist of a woman:
his wife's, his mistress's, perhaps the Queen's.
But the body of the air is Beatriz.

All night long we heard birds passing.

Tuesday, October 9

ALL NIGHT

Slaves to the vagaries of weather, displaced
by the pull of the earth, these are marionettes
who wait for the dark to lift their tails. They are
wary of land, the mountains that glare, the winds

that strip the forest of leaves. In the homing drive
they follow the summer south, migrants exposed,
vibrating the edges of air. They remember
the nest, the jut of the trees they were born on,

repeating every twist and turn of the journey;
the exodus of tanager and finch.
These are the faithful feathers and souls of distance:
they lower their flight over land, searching for seeds.

Night is a carousel. The sky wheels; last stars
shut down. The cadence of dawn at sea is thick
with purling, the terrible whistle of wings.
Birds know where they are and where they have

to go. They carry a crystal between their skulls
and their softer bones. Their eyes are immovable,
dense as stars. At noon, the sun in the south
is the axis. Their beaks align with light.

Between day and night I made 59 leagues. I told the crew 44 leagues, but they could no longer stand it; they complained of the long voyage and I added that it was useless to complain since I had come to find the Indies and thus had to continue the voyage until I found them.

Wednesday, 10 October

MUTINY

Exhausted from the constant flex of courage,
he breathes and the air grows dark. Hot beneath
the armor he invents, he is as cautious
as a cat. The men grow bold. They march in

circles, insecure among the masts.
They scheme. They murmur and they sneer. They gather
on deck in herds like lowing cows. The ships
are full of leaks and faults, and casks are running

short of wine. He has tricked them with his
demons and his science. His nerve has brought them
out too far. Undone by every shadow,
the men sigh and hiss like trees in drought.

But he finds in their convoluted anger
something of a dolphin's grace. He tries
to speak, but they aren't listening and his throat
is parched. He opens the clasp of his collar,

feels his own death throbbing in his fingers.
He is by far their better sailor, and he
will take them as they are: rude, inconstant,
and ungrateful, into the promised land.

At 10 o'clock at night, while standing on the sterncastle, I thought I saw a light to the west. It looked like a little wax candle bobbing up and down.

Thursday, 11 October

A LIGHT

He cannot trust his senses: light is uncertain;
he thinks of steadfast things: the drone of water,
vermin that spawn in the slop and stench of the hold.
No one is sleeping. The men crowd the deck

with prayer. They pace. They scan the dark. Night
is a herd of bulls. What if there is no light?
Once, wrecked, he swam on an oar six hours,
pushing himself toward the silver brooch of land.

All night he steered himself by stars. Now
the moon comes full, unstiffening the ships:
the men are sweating, the sea is rough and tumbled
with branches, herbage, stones. The sails are beating

like wings. The tattered reed of the coastline
is breaking the backs of the waves, as if
water had come far enough. The world revolves
in melancholy circles. Tonight, the sky

is a totem, an inlet of fears. An island
drags the compass by degrees. On the lip
of the horizon, fire. He can see the flame,
round as the back of a turtle and as strong.

Then, at two hours after midnight, the land appeared.

Friday, 12 October

LANDFALL

Flotsam of branches; flotsam of wildest rose.
The vague hills begin to reveal themselves.
His line of sight is poised between the stars
that promise everything and the ships that groan.

The windlass sighs. He is surprised to find
regret. Here is the end of desire:
a spit of land snaking north. The wind
is beating the cliffs into mouths. The island

that rises has too many lagoons. No route
is perfect. There are always errors in living,
in leeway and drift. His heart is a prairie;
his mind, a masterplan. A new world is

yet to be invented: should he create
or divide? Invisible shoals take refuge
in the moonlight. The sea is his mother:
not for what she gives but what she holds.

He has sailed ten lines into the hemisphere
of ruin. Did he think he would discover
something less? Now is the arming of courage:
the sands are rolling; the waves raping the land.

*At dawn we saw naked people, and
I went ashore in the ship's boat, armed.*

Friday, 12 October

GUANAHANÍ

White laurel. White parrots. The lanterns
swell and preen. Light pours from the hills
like just-cut grass. He feels the urge to comb
his matted hair, to rub away the smudge

and circumstance, the oils that stain. He wants
to appear to them as the phoenix from the sky.
He has seen the Moorish King march through the gates
of Granada, vanquished. He has seen him weep.

He, too, has fattened the belly of property:
it will be easy to overthrow this harbor.
He carries the sword of friendship in its sheaf.
He'll take the people with glass beads and bells.

The natives swim in the gun-metal water.
They paddle out in dugouts to give up their spears.
Their gifts: fish teeth and balls of thread. They reach
out their hands to stroke the marvelous beards.

These are a people of reefs, a people of shallows.
Their hair is feathers. Land is their bread, and land
is the God who feeds them. They speak like the river;
they paint their faces red. They will bathe in dust.

All of them go around as naked as their mothers bore them; and the women also, although I did not see more than one very young girl.

Friday, 12 October

THE GIRL

A girl is watching. The men in boots come
and go from the ships in droves. Her naked skin
is shining. Her eyes close into perfect moons.
From where she stands, the bottom of the sea

is visible: the water is clean under
the lee of land. The trees, past green, deliver
their fruit to ripeness. She is the harvest.
The sun performs its sacraments for her.

She wades in the solace of water; the shore
is a necklace of shells and unseen stars.
She opens her eyes before the spread of light.
A full moon is stirring. The island speaks

for itself: no Golden Khan, no spices, no cloves.
Dusk is a silhouette of birds against
the dark. The feet of the girl are buried. She is
the world incarnate; she is the old and the new.

Night comes swiftly as a falcon. The island
stills. The girl is kneeling in sand. She cups
her hands in water to wash her face. The sea
becomes less salty. All of her tears are returned.

CODA

They should be good
and intelligent servants;
for I see that they say
very quickly
everything that is said to them;
and I believe that they
will become Christian
very easily, for it seems to me
that they have no religion.
Our Lord pleasing,
at the time of my departure
I will take six of them from here
to your Highnesses
in order that they may learn to speak.

—from the *Diario* of
Christopher Columbus
Friday, 12 October 1492

NOTES

ON *THE* DIARIO *OF CHRISTOPHER COLUMBUS*

In the prologue to his journal of what he called "The First Voyage of Discovery," Christopher Columbus wrote: *I thought of writing on this whole voyage, very diligently, all that I would do and see and experience,* and history tells us that he did. But both his handwritten journal of the Atlantic crossing, presented to Ferdinand and Isabela on his return to Spain, and the one complete copy of that manuscript have been lost for centuries.

But portions of the record remain. Bartolomé de Las Casas, a cleric whose father and uncle sailed on the Second Voyage (1493–96) and who came to the colony himself in 1502, made *The Book of the First Navigation,* an abstract of a copy of the original journal. And in 1527 he began his *History of the Indies.* Translated (only in portion; to date there is no complete English version) by Andrée Collard (Harper and Row, 1971), this *History* quotes from and partially summarizes the journal. At about the same time that Las Casas was writing, Ferdinand, the youngest son of Columbus, was preparing a biography of his father. The original Spanish manuscript is lost, but a 1571 Italian version has been translated by Benjamin Keen (Rutgers University Press, 1959) as *The Life of the Admiral Christopher Columbus by His Son,* and comprises memories of the voyages (Ferdinand accompanied his father on the Fourth Voyage); insights into the personality of Columbus; what seem to be fanciful anecdotes; as well as quotations from the original journal. These three texts are all that remain of the actual language of the Admiral's accounts.

Each of the poems in this collection represents an entry in the *Diario de a bordo,* the onboard log of the outward passage of the First Voyage across the Atlantic, and each begins with a citation from the log Columbus wrote aboard the *Santa María.* For the most part, the epigraphs are quoted from *The Log of Christopher Columbus,* translated and reconstructed by Robert H. Fuson (International Marine, 1987). In some cases, the quotations are compilations of Fuson's work and *The Diario of Christopher Columbus 1492–1493,* transcribed and translated by Oliver Dunn and James E. Kelley (University of Oklahoma Press, 1988); and also *The Journal of the First Voyage,* translated by John Boyd Thatcher (Putnam, 1903), and *Journals and Other Documents of the Life and Voyages of Christopher Columbus,* translated by Samuel Eliot Morison (Heritage, 1963).

BEFORE SUNRISE

Iam lucis orto sidere: "Now at the rising star of light." These are the opening words of the prayer they heard. The ships departed before dawn, on 3 August, the deadline for the expulsion of the Jews from Spain. The edict of expulsion was made by Ferdinand and Isabela on 30 March 1492, and it set the time limit of 31 July, but the Queen extended it by three days. After midnight on 2 August no Jew was permitted to live in Spain. Salvador de Madariaga (*Christopher Columbus,* Macmillan, 1940) is the first of several scholars to argue that the date of departure is a key in the evidence proving that Columbus was of Jewish descent. Other scholars disagree.

TO THE CANARIES

They headed southwest by south toward the Canary Islands so that they might sail from there due west to Asia. At the time of this voyage, Spain had taken only two of the seven islands in the archipelago and the land was considered a wilderness.

Columbus had read the works of Pliny, who describes the Canaries in considerable detail in *Natural History,* Book VI: 37.

BREAKING DOWN

Ferdinand's *Historie* explains at length how Columbus suspected that someone had tampered with the *Pinta*'s rudder. He reports that Columbus suspected the ship's owner. What is important in this event is that now the fleet would have to land in the Canaries, where Columbus would try to find a new ship.

Considerable controversy surrounds the nationality of Columbus. Scholars argue that he was either Italian, Corsican, Spanish, or Portuguese.

BECALMED

From 11 August through 5 September, I am exclusively quoting Fuson, who reconstructs the *Diario* for those days. Columbus was sailing among the islands and much of what actually happened was not written down. By the time of this poem, Columbus has sent the *Pinta* to Gran Canaria, where there are forests enough to fix a rudder, while the *Santa María* and the *Niña* head for Gomera to get provisions.

AT ANCHOR

Hierro is the last and most westerly island in the chain.

The frescoes remain in the Iglesia de Magdalena in Seville.

GOMERA

The Guanche were a stone age people living on Gomera in the time of the conquistadors.

He left his son, Diego, at La Rábida, the Franciscan monastery near Palos. Diego's mother, Doña Felipa Perestrella, was the wife of Columbus. She died in Portugal when the boy was four. The next year Columbus and the boy left for Spain. In 1488 a second son, Ferdinand, was born to Beatriz Enrique de Harana in Córdoba. He was living with his mother at the time of his father's First Voyage.

The "whistling tongue" is *silbo* and is still spoken on the island. In our times, the vocabulary has been reduced to two thousand words.

AT GRAN CANARIA

"disturbed somewhat": this is the first of the allusions to his troubles with Martín Alonso Pinzón, captain of the *Pinta*. The captain of the *Niña* was his brother. The competition and ill will between the family Pinzón and the family Columbus raged for a century after the voyage.

"the wound": historians tell us that Columbus was shot in 1477, in a battle off the coast of Portugal. When his bones were moved from the Cathedral in Seville to be buried again in the Cathedral Primada de América in Santo Domingo, the Dominican Republic, gunshot was found in his tomb.

FIXING THE RUDDER

Maestro Diego is the boatswain on the *Santa María*.

RERIGGING THE NIÑA

The lateen, triangulated sails of the *Niña* are considered too cumbersome for the voyage. To better catch the full force of the trade winds, Columbus wants them changed to the same square rig as the *Pinta* and the *Santa María*.

Sagres is the westernmost city of Portugal, which, in 1492, was considered the end of the known world.

THE DOUBLE RECKONING

He maintains two reckonings until 10 October, the day before landfall. The daily journal entries include both sets of figures. In actuality, Columbus had overestimated the distance between the continents and, as it turned out, the second "untrue" figures proved to be the more accurate.

THE BRANCH OF FIRE

Columbus learned about meteorites by reading Ptolemy's *Tetrabiblos*, II, and Seneca's *Naturales Quaestiones*, II.

FALSE LANDFALL

There were actually two false sightings of land. Columbus placed very heavy monetary penalties on any man who said he saw land when he hadn't.

RAIN

A caravel is a type of small sailing vessel with a broad bow, high poop, and lateen sails. Both the *Niña* and the *Pinta* were caravels, while the larger *Santa María* was a three-masted, square-rigged *nao*, or ship.

CIPANGO

Cipango is Japan. Columbus learned the customs of Cipango by reading Marco Polo's *Travels*.

THE TOKEN

A gromet or *grumete* is an ordinary seaman or ship's boy.

BREEZES

The Guadalquivir is the river that runs through Seville to the sea. In the thirteenth century, twin towers, built by the Moors on its opposite banks, were joined by a heavy chain that served to control passage.

A LIGHT

He writes that he saw a light at 10 o'clock that evening; but the actual firing of the cannon to signal landfall was not made until two hours later, in response to the shouts of a seaman, Rodrigo de Triana, of the *Pinta*. The Spanish Crown had offered an annuity of 10,000 *maravedis* to the first sailor to sight land, and it was Columbus who claimed the reward.

LANDFALL

This and the two subsequent poems take place on the same day.

There is an active controversy among geographers about the actual location of the landfall. Most prominently, Joseph Judge for the National Geographic Society claims that the island is Samana Cay, in the Bahama group, while Mauricio Obregón argues that San Salvador or Watlings Island is the actual site.

"ruin": from this journey onward, the life of Columbus was a trial of rebuke. In 1506, after three more voyages to the Americas (islands that he continued to believe were the Indies), he died repudiated: stripped of rank and privilege, banished from what he called "the second world," ill and unaware of the success of his discovery of a sailing route to the West.

GUANAHANÍ

Columbus renames the island San Salvador. Guanahaní is its native name.

THE GIRL

At the end of the fifteenth century, before the arrival of the Columbus expedition, the Arawak people of the Taino tribe thrived in the Antilles and Bahama Islands. Modern scholars disagree about their number: estimates of the original Taino population range from ten thousand to as many as eight million. In any case, by the turn of the next century there were none.

Barbara Helfgott Hyett's first book of poems, *In Evidence: Poems of the Liberation of Nazi Concentration Camps,* was selected *Booklist*'s "Editor's Choice" in 1986. Her second collection, *Natural Law,* was published in 1989. Her poems have appeared widely in such magazines as *The Nation, The New Republic, The Massachusetts Review, Poetry Northwest, The Women's Review of Books,* as well as in a number of anthologies. The recipient of a Massachusetts Artists Fellowship in Poetry, her other awards include grants to travel in Spain, Portugal, and the Canary Islands to conduct research on the First Voyage of Columbus. A seasoned teacher and lecturer, Helfgott Hyett is preceptor of English at Boston University. She lives with her family in Brookline, Mass.

Library of Congress Cataloging-in-Publication Data

Hyett, Barbara Helfgott.
    The double reckoning of Christopher Columbus, 3 August–
12 October 1492 : poems / by Barbara Helfgott Hyett : with a fore-
word by Robert H. Fuson.
        p.   cm.
    ISBN 0-252-01866-4
    1. Columbus, Christopher—Poetry.   2. America—Discovery
and exploration—Spanish—Poetry.   I. Title.
PS3558.E4744D68 1992
811'.54—dc20   91-28062
                    CIP

28 Days
DATE DUE

GAYLORD			PRINTED IN U.S.A.